The Cartographer
नक़्शानवीस

Mohan Rana

The Cartographer
नक़्शानवीस

Translated from Hindi by
Lucy Rosenstein with Bernard O'Donoghue

poetry
translation
centre

First published in 2020
by the Poetry Translation Centre Ltd
The Albany, Douglas Way, London, SE8 4AG

www.poetrytranslation.org

Poems © Mohan Rana 2020
English Translations © Lucy Rosenstein and Bernard O'Donoghue 2020
Introduction © Lucy Rosenstein 2020
Afterword © Alison Brackenbury 2020
Mohan Rana Photograph © Manuel Fernández Minaya

Some of these poems first appeared in *Poems* (Enitharmon; 2011).

ISBN: 978-1-9161141-4-2

A catalogue record for this book is available from the British Library

Typeset in Minion / Arial Unicode by Poetry Translation Centre Ltd

Series Editor: Edward Doegar
Cover Design: Kit Humphrey
Printed in the UK by TJ Books Limited

The PTC is supported using public funding by
Arts Council England

Contents

Introduction	7
Crossing Over	11
Of No Fixed Abode	13
Voice	17
To the Lost Children	21
Sleeping Awake	23
What is Seen	25
The Photograph	27
In the Shade of the Parasol Pine	29
Another Word for It	31
Did You Hear It Too?	33
After Midnight	35
The Colour of Water	37
Not What the Words…	39
As the Past Approaches	41

The Morning Post	43
The Evening News and the Roof of the World	47
In Your Own Words	51
The Cartographer	53
Reassurance	55
A Standard Shirt	57
Afterword	59
About the contributors	64
About the series	66

Introduction

The Indian poet, Mohan Rana, has lived in England for the past thirty years. Born in Delhi in 1964, he studied Humanities and went on to contribute poetry, reviews and articles on the arts to Hindi newspapers and magazines. Although based in England since 1990, he has continued to write and publish in his mother tongue, Hindi, producing eight highly-acclaimed collections of poetry, most recently *Shesh Anek* (*Much Remains*) in 2016.

Perhaps it is this distance from his native country that has contributed to his poems' most striking characteristic: their absolute refusal to accept anything at face value, their persistent – almost child-like – questioning of reality.

Yet behind this apparent naivety lies a deep layer of complex philosophical and literary inheritance. The quality of Advaita, or 'non-dualism' – the essence of the ancient scriptures of the Upanishads – permeates Rana's poetry, giving rise to its persistent questioning of identity, truth and reality. Other poems are influenced by Buddhism; for example, 'Not What the Words . . .' which, in its reflection on the creative process, suggests that meaning is not to be found in words themselves, but that it already inhabits the reader since, in Buddhism, reality has a cyclical nature. In this, the poem echoes the Buddhist doctrine of the chain of dependent origination: all experiences in life are processes subject to causation, this world being the last link in the chain of causation.

What gives Rana's poetry its magnetic quality is that, despite its philosophical profundity, his work is vividly accessible, even to those readers new to Indian philosophy and religion. His themes are universal and they are conveyed through simple, resonant images. Stars, birds and trees inhabit his poetry; and 'a standard shirt' features twice in this brief selection from his work. His poems are often preoccupied with rain – as in 'The Colour of Rain', 'After Midnight', 'Not What the Words . . .' – since he is fascinated by the idea of water as a repository of collective memory.

Rana's deep engagement with the notion of memory is inflected by his complex relationship with India: the country of his birth, his childhood and the language of his poetry, but which is now beyond his everyday geography. However rather than sinking into the sands of nostalgia, his work crafts a complex relationship with memory and time. Poems like 'After Midnight' and 'As the Past Approaches' address his notion of time, in which the future is a past we have yet to experience.

The tension between memory and oblivion, the acute awareness of the transient nature of life ('To the Lost Children', 'The Colour of Rain'), together with the irrepressible urge to seek the truth of existence and to recognise the unexpected quality of 'the ordinary', creates a sense of restlessness which is central to Rana's poetry. Indeed, in 'Did You Hear It Too?', 'your restlessness' is the protagonist of the poem itself. Mohan Rana's poetic sensibility is that of a traveller. It is the journey that engages him, not just the destination, since he prefers to take 'the road that leads nowhere' ('Not What the Words...'). Like one of his most famous predecessors, the founder of modernism in Hindi poetry, Agyeya, Rana is 'not even a traveller, but a seeker of a path'. Perhaps this is the secret behind the popularity of his poetry: it takes his readers on a journey of discovery that frees us of received meanings and reveals the extraordinary in the everyday.

Lucy Rosenstein

Poems

पारगमन

पिताजी के लिए

मैं अतीत था फिर भी मैं सबको भूल जाऊँगा
मैं सब सुन लेता हूँ अब, मैं अनहद हो गया हूँ
दूर तक देख लेता अब, मैं क्षितिज हो गया हूँ
सबसे दूर चला गया मैं, अगोचर इतना पास कि
एक हो गया हूँ अब तुम्हारी सांस में,
मिट्टी का पुतला मैं मिट्टी हो गया हूँ।

Crossing Over

For my father

I used to be the past myself, but I will still
Forget everyone. Now I hear everything,
Having become the music of the spheres.
And I can see far away now, I am the horizon.
Having gone so far away, no pace perceived,
I am so close to you, I share your breath.
A figure formed from dust, I have become dust.

अनिकेत

सः पर्यगात् – ईशोपनिषद् , श्लोक 8

बरस कितने बीते यहाँ इधर
वहाँ वे कहते फिर सुनाते कहानी
याद जिसे कभी करते जब तब
हम आपको याद करते हैं मैं सुनकर जैसे भूलता
धमनियों में बहते वर्तमान के तनाव को,
वे कठिन दिन अब दवा की तरह काम करते हैं ;
घर की रंगाई पुताई हो रही है बदलते मौसम में
और यह तैयार होगा बाज़ार में बिक्री के लिये
विश्वास की कीमत पर प्रॉपर्टी डीलर की खिड़की में

रोवन के पेड़ पर झींसी बारिश में रॉबिन बोलती
चुपचाप अपनी गाँठें खोल रहा है वसंत अभी,
अंतःकरण में विगत यात्राओं से
जाने क्या खोल रख देगा वह अपनी गठरी से कोंपलों के साथ

कवि पार चला जाता है...
उपनिषद कहते हैं - सीमा पार करता है कवि

अब कौन सी सीमा यह
शब्द की सीमा
प्रेम की सीमा
भय की सीमा
मौन की सीमा
पार करता
वह एक लावारिस जगह का निवासी पूछता,
दो खिड़कियाँ उसके हाथ में इस ओर उस ओर

Of No Fixed Abode

It is He that has gone abroad – Isha Upanishad, Verse 8

How many years have passed this way,
He says, and tells the story again
Which he recalls from time to time.
We remember you: hearing this it seems
I forget the present that flows through my veins.
Those hard days are healing now.
The house is being refurbished season by season,
To be ready for sale in the marketplace
In the estate agent's window at the price of trust.

Through the mist on the Rowan tree a robin speaks.
Spring quietly opens its parcel now,
Delivered from the inner journeys of the past.
Who knows what it will bring from its parcel, what buds.

The poet crosses over –
The Upanishads say – the poet crosses the border.

So what is this border,
The border of the word,
The border of love,
The border of fear,
The border of silence?
Crossing.
He, resident of an unclaimed place
With two windows, one on each side

दो दृश्य एक साथ अनिकेत आमने सामने
जैसे मैं और तुम उपस्थित हमेशा हर पंक्ति में कविता की

कि इस निगहबानी उड़ान में गोचर धरती आकाश में नहीं रहता
   अंतर,
शायद किसी को मालूम हो वह पता
अपने से बतकही उद्वेल में चलती रहती है आजीवन छँटाई बुनाई
और कल के बाक़ी वायदों के क़र्ज़ का निपटान,
कल कहा था आज फिर
जो बचा रह जाय उसे अपनी किताब में लिख देना,
तो मैं वापस सीमा पार करता हूँ
अपनी ही परछाईं पार करता,
यहाँ दो पैर बेनामी अलख सीमा को

मेरी आस्था है कविता में किन्तु विश्वास नहीं रहा भाषा पर
जैसे नहीं रहा अपनी हथेली की भाग्य रेखा पर।

Looking out on two stateless places:
Like you and me, present in every line of poetry.

In this reconnaissance flight, no distance between earth and sky.
Someone may know the address
In the turmoil of conversation the sorting and weaving
Goes on by itself all life long,
And the debts of the past and its commitments are paid again.
It was said yesterday, said again today
So write in your book whatever still remains.
I cross back over the boundary,
Passing my own shadow on the way.
In two steps I cross here a nameless, invisible boundary.

I have faith in poetry, but my trust in language is gone:
Gone with the line of fate inscribed in my palm.

आवाज़

एक दिन अचानक मैंने जाना
वो दरवाज़ा जिसे मैं अपने घर का पता समझता आया
उसे बैंक ने मॉर्गेज़ किया हुआ है,
वह दुनिया के लिए दरअसल बाहर जाने का प्रवेश द्वार था,
एक दीवार जिसकी नींव पर लगा था डिपॉज़िट बॉक्स मेरे पुरखों का

एक दिन अचानक मैंने जाना
जीवन में केवल एक बात पक्की है – आश्चर्य
अपना परिचय देते अब अपने इसी मंत्र को जपते
गले लगाता हूँ नए दोस्तों को जो मुझे याद नहीं करना चाहते,
कि नई पारिस्थितिकी में जहाँ सब कुछ कच्चा रास्ता
मैं खोजता अपने को याद रखने के लिए लिखता शब्द जिनमें
कभी भी बदल सकता है भूगोल अपनी सीमाएँ

अपनी कविता पर आशा कर भरोसा रखते
लोक कथा के प्यासे कौवे की तरह भटकता भीषण गरमी में
कि मैं पी सकूँ कुछ बूँदें मटके के तल से
बटोरता कंकड़ों को रेत के ढूहों से,
मैं कहता कि यह सब घटता हुआ सपना है मेरे दोस्त
उस नामाक़ूल नजूमी की तरह
जिसे कभी मालूम नहीं रहता अपने भविष्य के क़दमों का नक़्शा

एक बार पढ़ कर रख देता हूँ जो किताब अब ध्यान नहीं रहती
याद दिलाने के लिए नहीं रहता मुड़ा हुआ कोना उस किताब में
बचा नहीं कोई पन्ना जिसमें कोना बाकी हो
मोड़ कर रखने किए

Voice

One day suddenly I realized
That the door I have come to think of
As my own front door, was mortgaged to the bank.
In reality it was the exit to the world,
Through a wall in whose foundations
The deposit box of my ancestors was kept.

One day suddenly I realized
Only one thing is certain in life – the unpredictable.
I rediscover this truth when I make new friends
And embrace those who do not want to know me.
In the new ecology where all is an unclaimed road
Where I can't find myself, I must remember to write
Words for a geography that can always change its borders.

I place my hope in poetry, depend on that
Like the inventive thirsty crow, as I wander in this terrible heat
So I can drink a few drops from the depths of this clay jug,
Gathering pebbles from its mound of sand.
All this, my friend, is a dream that has come to pass,
As the failed fortune-teller
Can never map out his future steps.

I leave the book which does not hold my attention
With no corner folded to tell me where I've got to.
But there is no page whose corner is not turned down,

जैसे अपने खड़े होने के लिए पैर भर जगह,
जहाँ से मैं रह पाऊँ निर्भय इन शब्दों के बीच अपने आप को

गर मुझे मालूम होता यह मसिजीवी चोला
किसी और का है
कुछ और पहन कर निकल पड़ता किसी अच्छे दिन
और संभव होता तो बदल लेता जीवनी के उस तैयार प्रारूप को चुपचाप
आपसी लेन देन में बिना ताज़ा भाव सोचे हर दिन उसी आकाश को
    बदलते,
आमने सामने चौंक कर जान लेते यक-बारगी अपनी बदली सूरत,
पलट कर सुन पाता तुम्हारी आवाज़ फिर
एक दिन मैंने पहचाना

No space among the words of which
I can take my confident stand without dread.

If I had known this writer's garb is someone else's,
I'd have worn something else for this fine day
If it were possible I'd have silently changed
This conventional version of my biography.
For the ordinary give and take of every day,
I might have substituted sky.
Suddenly brought face to face, I'd have been startled
To recognize the voice as yours,
For once remembering whose it was.

खोए बच्चों के नाम

एक चिट्ठी मैं लिखना चाहता हूँ खोए बच्चों के नाम
शहतूत की टहनियों से टँगे
छोटे होते जाते हैं उनके कपड़े
फैलती हैं टहनियाँ
घना होता जाता है शहतूत
और सालों में कभी एक बार मैं बूढ़े पेड़ को देखता हूँ
अपनी छाया पर झुके हुए,
तार-तार होते जाते हैं कपड़े
उनकी स्मृतियाँ हवा में मिलती हैं पानी
में घुलती हैं मौसमों में डूबती हैं
महीन होती जाती भूली हुई कविता सी

मैं लिखना चाहता हूँ अपने बारे में पर
किसी और की कहने लगता हूँ
समकालीन पुराने हो जाते हैं,
एक दिन वे खो जाएँगे
खोए हुए बच्चों की तरह एक दिन
एक दिन खो जाएगा - कई दिनों में कहीं

एक चिट्ठी मैं लिखना चाहता हूँ
खोए हुए बच्चों के नाम
खोए हुए बचपन की ओर से

To the Lost Children

I want to write to the lost children,
those whose clothes hung from the branches
of the mulberry tree, getting smaller
as the branches grew.
The tree gets thicker and thicker
until years later I see the old tree
bent over its own shadow.
The clothes turn to shreds;
their memories mix in the wind,
dissolve in water, sink under the seasons,
fade like a forgotten poem.

I set out to write about myself
but I start talking of someone else.
My contemporaries are growing older.
One day they too will go missing
like the lost children: one day.
One day will go missing out of many.

I want to write a letter
to the lost children
posted from their lost childhood.

सोते जागते

यहीं कहीं जो रह जाता फिर वहीं
भूल कर याद रह जाता

मैंने रोपा था उखड़े पेड़ की छाया को
आकाश के संताप को अपने सीने पर
सांस भर एक दम

उन आलिंगनों में लिपटी छायाएँ
हिलती दोपहर छू कर वह सुनती धड़कन,
तुम्हारा स्पर्श मेरी हथेली पर

भूल कर याद रह जाता हर दिन
यहीं जो रह जाता फिर और कहीं

Sleeping Awake

What survives somewhere here, once forgotten,
Is remembered day after day somewhere else.

I had planted the shade of the uprooted tree,
The sky's anguish in my breast,
Drawing a single breath.

Shadows wrapped in those embraces,
Trembling at noon. She listens to my heart beating,
Your touch on my palm.

What survives somewhere here, once forgotten,
Is remembered day after day somewhere else.

क्या नहीं देखा

पीले फूलों की झाड़ी में
टंगी काठ की मछली
मंडराती मूंदे अपनी आँखें
देखती सपना
आकाश में उड़ते कपासी बादलों में
उमड़ती हैं लहरों की स्मृतियाँ

क्या नहीं देखा मैंने
जिसे सोचा कभी किसी ने
पीले फूलों को देख,
क्या उसने मुझे भी देखा
उन टहनियों के बीच
पीले फूलों की झाड़ी में

What is Seen

In the bush of yellow flowers
A wooden fish hangs
Turning. Its closed eyes
See a vision:
In the cotton clouds high in the sky
Rise the memories of waves

What did I not see
Which someone thought of at some time
Seeing those yellow flowers?
Did the fish also see me
Amongst the branches
In the bush of yellow flowers?

फ़ोटोग्राफ़ में

दोनों ओर जंगल बीच रास्ता रोशनी और दिशा के साथ
दोनों ओर जंगल कहकहाता बीच रास्ता शांत
दोनों ओर जंगल चीख़ता बीच रास्ता विरक्त
दोनों ओर जंगल सपनों में डूबा बीच रास्ता यह विमुक्त किसी नींद से
हिलता यह दृश्य आँखों में जैसे पानी की सतह पर कोई प्रतिबिम्ब,
चौंकता चेहरा झुका हुआ उस पर
बंद गीली आँखों में
डबडबाती एक दुनिया,
दिशासूचक की तरह ले जाता
तुम्हारे भीतर प्रेम किसी अनजाने रास्ते पर तुम्हें
और सच कर देता है मुक्त,
खोल दो अपनी बंद हथेलियों को
हवा नहीं छुप सकती उनमें
रोशनी भी नहीं
वे ख़ुद को ही कैद किए हुए हैं इस जेल में,
देखना चाहता हूँ तुम्हारा चेहरा
किसी अकस्मात से पहले

The Photograph

Woods on either side: light along the path down the middle.
Woods on either side and loud laughter: path silent down the middle.
Woods on either side, and screams: path unmoved down the middle.
Woods on either side, bathed in dreams: the path released from sleep.

This vision trembles on the eyes like the mirroring surface of water.
A face bent over it is startled
at the world shimmering
in those shut, moist eyes:
like a compass, the love inside you
takes you on an unfamiliar path
and the truth releases you.

Open out your clenched palms.
The wind can't hide inside them,
nor light either.
They have made their own prison.
I want, suddenly, to see your face:
then to be surprised.

छतनार चीड़ की छाया में

थक कर बैठ जाती है दोपहर
इन बिसूरती गरमियों एड्रियाटिक की मंथर करवटें
मैं भूल जाना चाहता हूँ वे सारे वायदे
तपते भूगोल की त्वचा पर गुमसुम,
मुझे मालूम है वे पूरे नहीं हो सकते
कि वे झूठ हैं
कि वह सच है मेरा ही अपना
कि मैं आश्वस्त करता हूँ ख़ुद को ही
कि बेचैन सरसर हवा में पकता
तैयार हो रहा है पतझर जुलाई के धूसरित कदमों,
अपनी भाषा से मिला मुझे एक शब्दकोश
जिसमें प्रेम के कई पूरक हैं
उतने ही भय के
उसके मुड़े तुड़े पन्नों में,
अपने चेहरे की रेखाओं में एक पहचान
पर तुम्हारा नाम याद नहीं आता अब

In the Shade of the Parasol Pine

Grown weary at midday in the grievous heat,
By the tiring waves of the Adriatic
I want to forget all those empty promises
Burned onto the quiet contours of the skin.
I know that they will never become real,
That they are lies and the only truth
Is this restless, rustling air,
As I remind myself that autumn
Ripens under the arid footpaths of July.
In the dictionary of my private language
There are enough entries for love and fear
Amid its well-thumbed pages to make plain
The lines of my ageing face, even though
I don't remember your face any more.

होगा एक और शब्द

नीली रंगतें बदलतीं
आकाश और लहरों की
बादल गुनगुनाता कुछ
सपना सा खुली आँखों का
कैसा होगा यह दिन
कैसा होगा
यह वस्त्र क्षणों का
ऊन के धागों का गोला
समय को बुनता
उनींदे पत्थरों को थपकाता

होगा एक और शब्द
कहने को
यह किसी और दिन

Another Word for It

Different blues
in sky and waves.
The cloud hums a dream
of eyes open.
So what will this day be like,
this garment of moments?
The ball of thread
that knits time
taps the sleepy stones.

There may be a better way
to say this
some other day.

क्या तुमने भी सुना

चलती रही सारी रात
तुम्हारी बेचैनी लिस्बन की गीली सड़कों पर
रिमझिम के साथ
मूक कराह कि
जिसे सुन जाग उठा बहुत सबेरे,
कोई चिड़िया बोलती झुटपुटे में
जैसे वह भी जाग पड़ी कुछ सुनकर

सोई नहीं सारी रात कुछ देखकर बंद आँखों से
चलती रही तुम्हारी बेचैनी
मेरे भीतर
टूटती आवाज़ समुंदर के सीत्कार में
उमड़ती लहरों के बीच,
चादर की तहों में करवट बदलते
क्या तुमने भी सुना उस चिड़िया को

Did You Hear It Too?

All night long your restlessness
walked the wet streets of Lisbon,
pitter-patter.
A silent moan
woke me at daybreak.
A bird
was singing in the dawn:
something had woken it up too.

All night long your restlessness,
unable to sleep, walked and peered
with eyes closed
inside me.
A sound broke in the ocean's sigh
amidst the rising waves.
Turning over in the sheets' folds,
did you hear the bird too?

तीसरा पहर

मैंने तारों को देखा बहुत दूर
जितना मैं उनसे
वे दिखे इस पल में
टिमटिमाते अतीत के पल
अँधेरे की असीमता में,
सुबह का पीछा करती रात में
यह तीसरा पहर

और मैं तय नहीं कर पाता
क्या मैं जी रहा हूँ जीवन पहली बार,
या इसे भूलकर जीते हुए दोहराए जा रहा हूँ
सांस के पहले ही पल को हमेशा

क्या मछली भी पानी पीती होगी
या सूरज को भी लगती होगी गरमी
क्या रोशनी को भी कभी दिखता होगा अंधकार
क्या बारिश भी हमेशा भीग जाती होगी,
मेरी तरह क्या सपने भी करते होंगे सवाल नींद के बारे में

दूर दूर बहुत दूर चला आया मैं
जब मैंने देखा तारों को - देखा बहुत पास,
आज बारिश होती रही दिनभर
और शब्द धुलते रहे तुम्हारे चेहरे से

After Midnight

I saw the stars far off -
as far as I from them:
in this moment I saw them -
in moments of the twinkling past.
In the boundless depths of darkness,
these hours
hunt the morning through the night.

And I can't make up my mind:
am I living this life for the first time?
Or repeating it, forgetting as I live
the first moment of breath every time?

Does the fish too drink water?
Does the sun feel the heat?
Does the light see the dark?
Does the rain too get wet?
Do dreams ask questions about sleep as I do?

I walked a long, long way
and when I saw, I saw the stars close by.
Today it rained all day long and the words were washed away
from your face.

पानी का रंग

जेन के लिए

यहाँ तो बारिश होती रही लगातार कई दिनों से
जैसे वह धो रही हो हमारे दाग़ों को जो छूटते ही नहीं
बस बदरंग होते जा रहे हैं क़मीज़ पर
जिसे पहनते हुए कई मौसम गुज़र चुके
जिनकी स्मृतियाँ भी मिट चुकी हैं दीवारों से

कि ना यह गरमी का मौसम
ना पतझर का ना ही यह सर्दियों का कोई दिन
कभी मैं अपने को ही पहचान कर भूल जाता हूँ

शायद कोई रंग ही ना बचे किसी सदी में इतनी बारिश के बाद
यह क़मीज़ तब पानी के रंग की होगी।

The Colour of Water

for Jane

Rain falling, day after day,
as if trying to clean off
our permanent stains,
but all it does is discolour
this well-worn shirt,
and wash the memory
of all the passing seasons
from the walls.

This is not summer
nor autumn nor winter:
sometimes I recognize myself,
then forget.

Maybe after so much rain
all colour will be washed out
and my shirt then be the colour of water.

अर्थ शब्दों में नहीं तुम्हारे भीतर है

मैं बारिश में शब्दों को सुखाता हूँ
और एक दिन उनकी सफ़ेदी ही बचती है
जगमगाता है बरामदा शून्यता से
फिर मैं उन्हें भीतर ले आता हूँ

वे गिरे हुए छिटके हुए क़तरे जीवन के
उन्हें चुन जोड़ बनाता कोई अनुभव
जिसका कोई अर्थ नहीं बनता
बिना कोई कारण पतझर उनमें प्रकट होता
बाग़ की सीमाओं से टकराता
कोई बरसता बादल,
दो किनारों को रोकता कोई पुल उसमें
आता जैसे कुछ कहने,
अक्सर इस रास्ते पर कम ही लोग दिखते हैं
यह किसी नक़्शे में नहीं है
कहीं जाने के लिए नहीं यह रास्ता

बस जैसे चलते-चलते कुछ उठा कर साथ लेते ही
बन पड़ती कोई दिशा
जैसे गिरे हुए पत्ते को उठा कर
कि उसके गिरने से जनमता कोई बीज कहीं

Not What the Words...

I dry out words in the rain
until one day all that is left
is whiteness. The verandah dazzles
with emptiness, so I take them back in.

These are the fallen, scattered shards of life.
I pick them up and fit them all together
to make a pattern whose meaning can't be made out,
though in autumn
the leaves still fall in their season.

A rainy cloud hits
the edges of the garden,
and a bridge that has held apart
two riverbanks
comes in as if to speak.

As a rule few people travel this road.
It features on no map,
this road that leads nowhere.
But when, out for a walk, I pick something up,
the track appears: just as, when a leaf falls,
a seed somewhere is born out of that falling.

आता हुआ अतीत

आता हुआ अतीत,
भविष्य जिसे जीते हुए भी
अभी जानना बाक़ी है

दरवाज़े के परे ज़िंदगी है
और अटकल लगी है मन में कि
बाहर या भीतर
इस तरफ़ या उधर
यह बंद है या खुला ?
किसे है प्रतीक्षा वहाँ मेरी
किसकी है प्रतीक्षा मुझे
अभी जानना बाक़ी है

एक क़दम आगे
एक क़दम छूटता है पीछे
सच ना चाबी है ना ही ताला

As the Past Approaches

As the past approached,
the future, even when you've lived it,
remains to be seen.

Behind that door
there is life. But guess!
Out or in?
This side or the other?
Closed or open?
Who's waiting for me there?
Who am I waiting for?
I have still to discover.

One foot forward,
one backward.
The truth is
neither key nor lock.

सुबह की डाक

सहारा से उड़ आई धूल रात में
महाद्वीपों को लाँघती गिरी इस शहर पर,
नहीं कोई बवंडर उड़ा लाया पास के खेतों से
शायद पहली बार मैंने ध्यान दिया धूल पर,
बिना देखे मैं जी लेता हूँ सारा जीवन
सब कुछ सामान्य है यहाँ सब कुछ वहीं
जहाँ उसे होना चाहिए
पक्षी आकाश में मनुष्य पैदल
और मछलियाँ स्याह गहराईयों में

इस कविता के लिए विशेष बनाए मुखौटे को पहने
आँख खोले में खड़ा हूँ खाली मंच पर लगातार बोलता
काँच के डिब्बे में अपना नाम
उपनाम कुलनाम छद्मनाम नाम पता आयु जन्म स्थान
 शिक्षा कोई रोज़गार
कई दिन हर दिन जब से खोली मैंने आँख,
टूटी हुई कठपुतली सा हिलता
टेढ़ा मेढ़ा उलझता धागों से
अपनी ही मुरझाहट में सिमटता
साँस के लिए चीखता
अजनमा पात्र

देहरी पे पड़ी डाक
पुरानी हो चुकी बिना पढ़ी
हर सुबह के साथ,
जहाँ से मैं बढ़ता कहीं और एक और दिन
निकलता उसे देख रुकता छाया की तरह पलभर
सुबह की डाक

The Morning Post

Sand has flown from the Sahara in the night,
crossing lands and seas to fall on this city.
Or has some wind blown it from nearby fields?
For the first time I take notice of dust:
all my life I have lived without seeing
all that is ordinary, all that is
where it should be:
birds in the sky, men on land,
fish in the sea's dark depths.

Wearing a mask
made specially for this poem,
I stand with eyes open on an empty stage,
declaiming inside a glass box
my name, nickname, surname, pen-name,
address, age, birthplace, education, job.
Every day since I opened my eyes
I have done this, trembling like a broken puppet
dangling from the strings
that grow twisted as I wither too,
gasping for breath,
my next role unwritten.
The post lies on the mat,
curling at the edges, unread
every morning.
From there I move on
another passing day: hardly a glance
at the morning post my figure shadows.

अपना ही होता है भूगोल दूरियों और निकटता का
तय करता जीवन के नियम सुख दुख
संकट का अंतराल और थोड़ा समय प्रेम के लिए,
मैं सीखता करता ग़लतियाँ मात्राओं की
छोटी बातों में पूरा होता मेरा दिन
अधूरे कामों को कल के छोड़ता अधूरा कल के लिए,
पुराना होता जाता अपने को नया बनाते
आज का कोट पहने

The geography of near and far inside you
decides what life brings: happiness or sorrow;
time of grief, a brief moment for love.
Over and over I practise the minor rules
of punctuation: life still spent
on small distinctions. Yesterday's
unfinished business still unfinished
tomorrow. I grow old, trying to become new
by wearing another coat today.

पार्क और शाम के समाचार और दुनिया की सबसे ऊँची छत

रोशनी कम हो रही है
कहीं और रोशनी हो रही है
हम शाम के ऊपर कर रहे हैं विचार
टहलते हुए पार्क के पेड़ों के बीच
जो खड़े हैं हाथ बाँधे गुमसुम,
कहीं बारिश हुई
ठंड हो गई यहाँ
हवा आते हुए साथ ले आई
थकी हुई आवाज़ें,
चलो लौट चलें
अँधेरा होने से पहले
रुककर हमने देखा रोशनी को
आकाश पर मिटते
काश हम एक ऊँची मीनार होते
देख पाते यह जाती कहाँ है आखिर
पर पोंछता हुआ इसे यह किसका हाथ है

आज शाम के मुख्य समाचार
आवंटित प्रसारण समय में
दुनिया अपना थका हुआ मुँह धोएगी
बिना महाकाव्य के समास हो जाएगी सदी
हम इन दिनों कोलाहल को सन्नाटे के दिन बिताएँगे,
एक समय था जब
दिन का उगना
शाम का डूबना कुछ सोचने की बात थी
वह पाषाण काल था जैसे कुछ देर पहले ही

The Evening News and the Roof of the World

While light for us is fading
elsewhere it is brightening.
We can think of the dusk
as we walk among the park trees
that stand still with arms folded.

Somewhere else there was rain
while here it grew colder.
The airs mingled to bring together
tired voices.
We must get home before dark.

We stopped to watch the light
being dusted from the sky,
and I want us to be a tall tower
to see round the horizon
whose hand it was that dimmed the light.

While we watch the official evening news
the world will wash its bleary face.
The century will end with no grand epic
though we will spend its final days of peace
to fanfares. There was a time
when the day's spring and the evening's fall
were something to think about:

सपने में मैंने देखा हम दुनिया की सबसे ऊँची छत पर थे
फिर भी तारे बहुत दूर थे
और अंतहीन था अँधेरा

as if the Stone Age was a short while ago.
Then in a dream I saw that, though we were
on the highest roof in the world,
the stars were still far away
and the darkness had no end.

अपनी कही बात

उन्होंने कहा न जाओ दुनिया के छोर तक
डर जाओगे अपनी लम्बी परछाईं को देख,
उस पार पंखों वाले अजगरों की दुनिया है
उनकी उगलती आग से उजली धरती
जहाँ न रात है न दिन अगर तुम पहुँचे तो
राह देखते पत्थर में बदल जाओगे,
जैसे किसी और से सुनी हो यह
अपनी कही बात
जीवन में रिहर्सल की संभावना होती तो
लिख रखे हैं पटकथा में कुछ परिवर्तन,
टाल नहीं सकता अपनी कही बात
लौटना
जाना
तुमसे प्रेम करना,
न लिखे कई दिनों तक,
पर मैं भला न था
बुरे दिनों को जीते मैं बुरा होता रहा
मैं समय की तरह अगोचर हो गया
घड़ी में घूमता लगातार
अपनी ही कही किसी बात पे सनकाया सा

In Your Own Words

They said: Don't go to the end of the Earth
because your lengthening shadow will frighten you.
There it is the world of winged pythons;
the earth there is ablaze with the fire they spit.
If you arrive where it is neither day nor night
you'll be turned into stone while you are waiting.

As if I had heard these words of mine
from somebody else.
If I'd had a full life rehearsal
I'd have made some changes to the text;
but I can't get away from my own words:
returning;
going away;
loving you.

But I wasn't good enough,
I couldn't write for days.
Living in evil times, I turned evil;
not seeing time passing,
I became imperceptible
as if trapped in clockwork
driven crazy by my own words.

नक़्शानवीस

पंक्तियों के बीच अनुपस्थित हो
तुम एक ख़ामोश पहचान
जैसे भटकते बादलों में अनुपस्थित बारिश,
तुम अनुपस्थित हो जीवन के हर रिक्त स्थान में
समय के अंतराल में
इन आतंकित गलियों में,
मैं देखता नहीं किसी खिड़की की ओर
रुकता नहीं किसी दरवाज़े के सामने
देखता नहीं घड़ी को
सुनता नहीं किसी पुकार को,
बदलती हुई सीमाओं के भूगोल में
मेरा भय ही मेरे साथ है।

The Cartographer

Between the lines it's you,
absent, but a silent presence
just as the rain is absent in the passing clouds.
There you are, absent, in every empty space
of life. In every gap of time
on these panic-stricken roads.
I don't look out any window,
I don't stop at any door
I don't watch the clock
I hear no one's call.
As geography changes its borders,
fear is my sole companion.

आश्वस्त

इस सरदी में मेरी परछाईं भी जम गई
मैं जागने की उम्मीद में था वसंत के आने पर
बुरी खबरों के समय में कुछ रोशनी की उम्मीद में
टहलते हुए अपनी उधेड़बुन मैं खोया चला जाता हूँ
सीले मोजों में सीलन सूखती ही नहीं
पैदल चलते भूलता चला जाता हूँ किसी अंतराल को,
फिर भी कुछ याद नहीं आता
कि हँस कर कहूँ अपने आप से
इतना कठिन तो नहीं झूठ बोलना
सच पर विश्वास करते हुए

Reassurance

In this cold my very shadow froze.
I had hoped to revive with the coming of spring:
Hoped for light in these dark times.
But as I walk, I remain in anguish
And my feet do not dry out with the season.
Walking onward I forget that time is passing.
Nothing comes to mind; and then I see it and smile:
'Making things up is not so difficult
So long as you believe in the truth.'

साधारण क़मीज़

दोपहर और शाम के बीच
आता है एक अंतराल
जब थक चुकी होती हैं
आवाज़ें क्रियाएँ

जैसे अब
समाप्त हो गईं सभी इच्छाएँ,
बैठ जाता हूँ किसी भी
ख़ाली कुर्सी पर

पीली क़मीज़ पहने
एक लड़का अभी गुज़रा
मुझे याद आई
अपनी क़मीज़
उन साधारण से दिनों में

यह संभव था
हाँ यह जीवन संभव था
मैं पहने हूँ अब भी
वैसी ही क़मीज़

A Standard Shirt

Between midday and nightfall
there comes a time
when the day's noise and actions
are already done with,

just as now,
all desires quenched,
I am ready to sit down
on any chair.

A boy in a yellow shirt
has just passed by
and made me think
of a shirt of mine
in those old ordinary days.

So it was possible.
Yes, this life was possible.
And here I am, still wearing
a shirt just like that.

Afterword

Simplicity in poetry is like water. There is a place for the black kick of coffee, a time for the gold-rimmed bubbles of champagne. But to live, we need water. Clarity is as refreshing as cool water. It is the feature of Mohan Rana's writing which struck me most powerfully at a first reading, together with its humility of tone: 'There may be a better way / to say this / some other day' ('Another Word for It'). I was also impressed by the absence of clutter in his poems. There are few place names, few period details, no long or crowded narratives. Very short lines recur, especially in the original Hindi. Quietly and unexpectedly, Rana's writing is sensitive to the different phases and lights of a day, to the seasons of a year, to time's long echoes, to the life of a vast and not always comfortable universe. Where temporalities can collapse, as he writes in 'The Evening News and the Roof of the World': 'as if the Stone Age was a short while ago[...] / the stars were still far away / and the darkness had no end.'

But Rana's work has an intensely human appeal. 'You' is a word which surfaces startlingly in the English translations of his poems, often in movingly direct lines, which seem also to speak to his reader: 'Turning over in the sheets' folds, / did you hear the bird too?' The person addressed (lover? friend?) is rarely identified. The poem's speaker may even admit 'I don't remember your face any more'. With disarming honesty, this speaker makes no claims to virtue:

> But I wasn't good enough,
> I couldn't write for days.
> Living in evil times, I turned evil
>
>   ('In Your Own Words')

The word 'border' is another haunting presence in Rana's work. Even without a biography, his reader might guess that these are the poems of a writer who knows two countries well, and often seems to speak from an emotional borderland between them: 'With two windows, one on each side / Looking out on two stateless places' ('Of No Fixed Abode').

His lines are alert to strange meetings, perhaps overlooked by his readers, between two very different landscapes: 'Sand has flown from the Sahara in the night' ('The Morning Post'). Movingly, his poems suddenly break back to weather and detail which recall India: 'as I wander in this terrible heat / So I can drink a few drops from the depths of this clay jug' ('Voice'). I particularly honour this poet's sensitivity to weather: a vital element in our lives, often ignored, especially in our cities, until savage variations reveal a crisis of climate...

One of Rana's most precious gifts is to enable his reader to re-view the familiar. When did you last notice dust? Here is Mohan Rana's reaction to that surprising Saharan sand:

> For the first time I take notice of dust
> all my life I have lived without seeing
> all that is ordinary, all that is
> where it should be

Awareness of the ordinary does not restrict our imagination but expands it. Rana's poetry leads its reader beyond everyday details into deeply thoughtful speculation about the life to which those days belong. 'The Morning Post', quoted above, might be expected, from its title, to concentrate on moments 'still spent / on small distinctions'. But the post is left 'on the mat, curling at the edges', while the poem, moving boldly into abstraction and clear, general statements, speaks of life, its seasons, 'happiness or sorrow', the past, age...

Disarmingly, the roving voice of Rana's poems does not claim assurance or extraordinary insight. It is the voice of a searcher, someone attentive to 'the fallen, scattered shards of life', whose efforts are strikingly self-aware: 'I pick them up and fit them all together / to make a pattern whose meaning can't be made out' ('Not What the Words...').

In a poem hauntingly named 'Of No Fixed Abode', Rana considers a line from the Hindu scriptures, the Upanishads. This classical line launches the poem into a series of intense questions:

> The Upanishads say – the poet crosses the border.
>
> So what is this border,
> The border of the word,
> The border of love,
> The border of fear,
> The border of silence?

The poet speaking in 'Of No Fixed Abode' does not assert, but question. The questions in Rana's poetry concern the deepest beliefs about human life. These beliefs may differ, in the world's major religions, but Rana's speculations link vividly to moments of experience which his readers are likely to have shared: 'am I living this life for the first time? / Or repeating it', he asks in 'After Midnight'.

His poems challenge conventional divisions between the animate and the inanimate, people and objects. The 'fish' described in 'What is Seen' is 'wooden', yet

> Did the fish also see me
> Amongst the branches
> In the bush of yellow flowers?

In the vision of Rana's poetry, our world, with its clutter, its personal anxieties and its troubling news, is revealed as far larger, stranger and – briefly – harmonious.

A wonderfully expansive quality of Rana's writing is its openness to the experience of others. His brief and mysterious poem, 'Sleeping Awake', is framed by two repeated lines: 'What survives somewhere here, once forgotten, / Is remembered day after day somewhere else.' This circling of a poem by repeated lines, deepening in meaning, is a device which I think is used too rarely in modern English poetry, but is powerfully present in its traditional song. There is a beautiful intensity, too, in Rana's opening account of a sunset, in 'The Evening News and the Roof of the World': 'While light for us is fading / elsewhere it is brightening'. Here is an emotional generosity – simple, but very hard-won – which I also hear in the final lines of Philip Larkin's 'Sad Steps':

> a reminder of the strength and pain
> Of being young; that it can't come again,
> But is for others undiminished somewhere.

Rana's poem ends with a moment when 'the darkness had no end'. There are points where his speaker seems to stare into the abyss, like the troubled voice of Edward Thomas' poems: 'Only an avenue, dark, nameless, without end' ('Old Man').

Against this backdrop, the insights in Rana's work are never glib. Like Larkin's, they are precious in their rarity. Here are the last three lines of 'The Colour Of Water', which unusually, has a dedication, 'to Jane':

> Maybe after so much rain
> all colour will be washed out
> and my shirt then be the colour of water.

This seems a fitting moment to pay tribute to the translation of these poems. Quite simply, I forgot almost entirely that the English words I was reading had been translated from Hindi, because I was absorbed by their ruefulness, urgency and insight. It is particularly appropriate for Rana's work, which is often cryptic, yet oddly transparent: 'the colour of water', anonymous, unpretentious, bravely open to the weather of the world, and of the heart. In the words of Joseph Brackett's Shaker Song, 'Simple Gifts', written in 1848:

> When true simplicity is gained,
> To bow and to bend we shan't be ashamed,
> To turn, turn will be our delight

What could be simpler, truly, than 'A Standard Shirt'? This is the poem of Rana's in which I find the deepest delight. The speaker, 'Between midday and nightfall', finds 'all desires quenched'. I recall Milton's final line in 'Samson Agonistes': 'And calm of mind, all passion spent'. I still remember these lines read to me, and my equally uncomprehending schoolmates, as a definition of 'catharsis', before, passionately, we rushed out of our Friday classroom... Rana's speaker glimpses a passerby, perhaps equally young, 'a boy in a yellow shirt'. This reminds him of his own past self 'in those old ordinary days'.

> So it was possible.
> Yes, this life was possible.
> And here I am, still wearing
> a shirt just like that.

So much can be found in this brief poem! It places a fleeting experience in time, first, within a day, then, in spreading circles, within a life. It is a quiet celebration of survival, of continuity despite change. Whether in time of calm or of crisis, it is, simply, a radiant moment: a gift. Mohan Rana's particular gift to his readers is of poetry which, as I have found, they may first like, then love.

Alison Brackenbury

Mohan Rana is a Hindi poet who grew up and studied in Delhi but now lives in Bath, England. His poetry explores the topics of identity, truth, memory and nature. He has published eight poetry collections, and with each book his reputation as a diaspora poet has grown. His latest collections are *Shesh Anek* (*Much Remains*), published in India by Copper Coin Publisher in 2016 and the trilingual e-book *Nekje Daleč Sem Uzrl Zvezde* (*I saw the stars far off*) published by Beletrina in 2020 in Slovenia. His poetry has been translated into several Indian and European languages.

Lucy Rosenstein graduated in Indology from Sofia University and obtained her MA and PhD in Hindi at SOAS, University of London, where she was a Lecturer for 10 years. She has published two books and numerous articles on Hindi poetry. Since 2007, the main focus of her work has been child and adolescent mental health, but she continues to be nurtured by her deep connection with poetry.

Bernard O'Donoghue was born in Cullen, Co Cork in 1945. He is an Emeritus Fellow of Wadham College, where he taught Medieval English and Modern Irish Poetry. He has published six collections of poetry, including *Gunpowder* (Faber; 1995), winner of the Whitbread Prize for Poetry, and, most recently, *The Seasons of Cullen Church* (Faber; 2016).

Alison Brackenbury was born in 1953. Her work has won Eric Gregory and Cholmondeley Awards, and has frequently been broadcast on BBC Radio. She has published ten collections. *Gallop*, her 2019 Selected Poems, is published by Carcanet.

About the Poetry Translation Centre

Set up in 2004, the Poetry Translation Centre is the only UK organisation dedicated to translating, publishing and promoting contemporary poetry from Africa, Asia and Latin America. We introduce extraordinary poets from around the world to new audiences through books, online resources and bilingual events. We champion diversity and representation in the arts, and forge enduring relations with diaspora communities in the UK. We explore the craft of translation through our long-running programme of workshops which are open to all.

The Poetry Translation Centre is based in London and is an Arts Council National Portfolio organisation. To find out more about us, including how you can support our work, please visit: www.poetrytranslation.org.

About the World Poet Series

The *World Poet Series* offers an introduction to some of the world's most exciting contemporary poets in an elegant pocket-sized format. The books are presented as bilingual editions, with the English and original-language text displayed side by side. The translations themselves have emerged from specially commissioned collaborations between leading English-language poets and translators. Completing each book is an afterword essay by a UK-based poet, responding to the translations.